SCIENCE OF FUN STUFF

Crayola! The Secrets of the Cool Colors and Hot Hues

by Bonnie Williams
illustrated by Rob McClurkan

Ready-to-Read

Simon Spotlight
New York   London   Toronto   Sydney   New Delhi

SIMON SPOTLIGHT

An imprint of Simon & Schuster Children's Publishing Division

1230 Avenue of the Americas, New York, New York 10020

This Simon Spotlight edition July 2018

For information about special discounts for bulk purchases, please contact Simon & Schuster Special Sales at 1-866-506-1949 or business@simonandschuster.com.
The Simon & Schuster Speakers Bureau can bring authors to your live event. For more information or to book an event contact the Simon & Schuster Speakers Bureau at 1-866-248-3049 or visit our website at www.simonspeakers.com.
Manufactured in the United States of America 0518 LAK

2 4 6 8 10 9 7 5 3 1

Library of Congress Cataloging-in-Publication Data

Names: Williams, Bonnie, author. | McClurkan, Rob, illustrator.

Title: The secrets of Crayola's cool colors and hot hues / by Bonnie Williams; illustrated by Rob McClurkan.

Description: New York : Simon Spotlight, 2018. | Series: Science of fun stuff | Series: Ready-to-read | Audience: Ages 6-8. | Audience: K to grade 3.

Identifiers: LCCN 2018002667 (print) | LCCN 2018002950 (ebook) | ISBN 9781534417755 (pbk) | ISBN 9781534417762 (hc) | ISBN 9781534417779 (eBook)

Subjects: LCSH: Color—Juvenile literature. | Crayons—Juvenile literature. | Color vision—Juvenile literature. | Crayola (Firm)—Juvenile literature.

Classification: LCC QC495.5 (ebook) | LCC QC495.5 .W557 2018 (print) | DDC 535.6—dc23

LC record available at https://lccn.loc.gov/2018002667

CONTENTS

CHAPTER 1
The Science Behind Crayons

Picture it. You have something in mind you'd like to draw. You take out a clean, unlined sheet of paper. You crack open the top of a box of Crayola crayons and see the flat points of the multicolored crayons, then smell that wonderful scent. You choose your first color, take the crayon out of the box, and make a smooth line of color on your paper.

Children around the world have been doing the same thing for well over 100 years since Crayola produced its first box of crayons in 1903. But how are Crayola crayons made? What ingredients are used to make them? And how do we even see color in the first place? By the end of this book you'll know the answers to these questions and more. You'll be a Science of Fun Stuff Expert on the colorful creation of crayons!

The magic starts with very pure paraffin wax and pigment. Paraffin wax is made from *petroleum*, an oil that comes from inside the earth. It does not have a color. So for crayons to be made, *pigment*—which is a fancy word for color—must be added. The pigment that Crayola uses comes in powdered form and is added to the melted wax. Today Crayola crayons come in 120 different colors.

Once the hot wax and colored powder have been mixed together, the liquid begins its journey through the factory assembly line. An *assembly line* is the order in which materials go through different machines or stations with workers to make a product. The colored wax is poured into crayon-shaped molds and cooled. It takes about five minutes for the crayons to cool. Then they are taken out of the molds and wrapped with labels. Each crayon is wrapped twice around with the label so that the crayon is extra

sturdy. Next the crayons get sorted by color. Once workers have inspected each crayon to make sure no points have been broken during this process, the perfect crayons are placed into boxes.

In addition to crayons, Crayola produces many markers, too. In fact, the company produces 465 million every year and came out with its first markers in 1978. It takes more ingredients to make a marker than a crayon (which is just the crayon and its label). A marker requires a plastic barrel printed with the Crayola logo and the color name, ink in a reservoir inside the barrel, a tip that allows the ink to come out of the reservoir, and a plastic cap.

Since 1988 Crayola has also made colored pencils. Today Crayola manufactures 600 million colored pencils each year. Colored pencils start with a wood casing made from trees. After the tree bark has been removed, the wood is treated, smoothed, and shaped so that color can be added. The color cores at the center of the pencils are created by mixing water, pigment, and extenders,

plus binding agents that hold everything together. This mixture is rolled out flat, then pressed into long, solid tube-like shapes called *cartridges*. Next they are cut into pencil-length pieces, dried, and placed on the wood. More wood is then added on top of the cartridge cores, and the two pieces of wood are glued tightly together. Then the wood is painted. Once the paint is dry, the pencils are sharpened and boxed up.

CHAPTER 2
Colorful Creations

So now that you know how these writing instruments are created, it's important that you understand how color is created. Life would be awfully dull if everything were black and white.

Crayola has 120 colors of crayons, and every single one of them is made from some combination of just three *primary colors*: red, blue, and yellow. The primary colors are the basics of the color wheel.

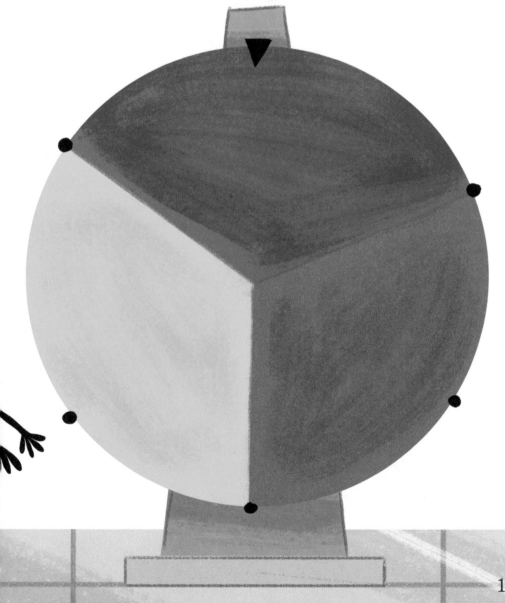

The next set of colors are known as *secondary colors*. They are made by a combination of equal parts red, yellow, or blue. So blue and red combined create violet. Blue and yellow combined create green. And yellow and red combined create orange.

Create a Color Lab!

Would you like to set up your own color laboratory? Here's what you need to do so:

- red, yellow, and blue food coloring
- water
- 3 clear containers
- 3 eyedroppers
- clear plastic wrap
- sheet of white paper

Fill each container with water. Add three drops of food coloring into each container so that you have a batch of red, yellow, and blue.

Place the piece of clear plastic wrap on top of the white paper.

Using the eyedroppers, drop the different colors onto the plastic wrap and create some colors!

Being an expert on something means you can get an awesome score on a quiz on that subject! Take this

SCIENCE OF CRAYOLA QUIZ

to see how much you've learned.

1. Parrafin wax is made from:
   a. sugar   b. petroleum   c. ultraviolet waves

2. The primary colors are:
   a. red, white, blue   b. red, yellow, black   c. red, yellow, blue

3. Crayola produced its first box of crayons in:
   a. 1903   b. 1978   c. 2013

4. The complementary color for violet is:
   a. gray   b. orange   c. yellow

5. The cone cells in your eyes sense:
   a. temperature   b. darkness   c. color

6. How many markers does Crayola produce each year?
   a. 465 million   b. 3 billion   c. 285,000

7. Ultraviolet light, X-rays, and gamma rays have wavelengths that are:
   a. shorter than violet   b. longer than red   c. the same length as black

8. The dominant hue for blue-green is:
   a. green   b. yellow   c. blue

Answers: 1. b 2. c 3. a 4. c 5. c 6. a 7. a 8. c